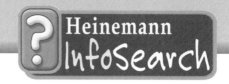

WHY SHOULD I LOOK AFTER MYSELF?

✦ and other questions about growing and health ✦

Heinemann
LIBRARY

Louise Spilsbury

www.heinemann.co.uk/library
Visit our website to find out more information about **Heinemann Library** books.

To order:
 Phone 44 (0) 1865 888066
 Send a fax to 44 (0) 1865 314091
 Visit the Heinemann Bookshop at www.heinemann.co.uk/library to browse our catalogue and order online.

First published in Great Britain by Heinemann Library, Halley Court, Jordan Hill, Oxford OX2 8EJ, part of Harcourt Education. Heinemann is a registered trademark of Harcourt Education Ltd.

Editorial: Nancy Dickmann, Jennifer Tubbs and Louise Galpine
Design: David Poole and Tokay Interactive Ltd (www.tokay.co.uk)
Illustrations: Kamae Design Ltd
Picture Research: Rebecca Sodergren and Liz Eddison
Production: Séverine Ribierre and Jonathan Smith

Originated by Ambassador Litho Ltd
Printed in China by Wing King Tong

ISBN 0 431 11098 0
07 06 05 04 03
10 9 8 7 6 5 4 3 2 1

British Library Cataloguing in Publication Data
Spilsbury, Louise
Why Should I Look After Myself? and other questions about growing and health
613
A full catalogue record for this book is available from the British Library.

Acknowledgements
Corbis pp. **5** (Chuck Savage), **7** (Reflections Photolibrary: Jenny Woodcock), **11** (Ed Bock), **15** (Layne Kennedy); Getty Images pp. **17**, **20**, **21**, **24**, **25** (Stone), **26**, **28** (Taxi); Liz Eddison p. **12**; PA Photos p. **10**; Photodisc pp. **4**, **8**; Science Photo Library pp. **9**, **14**, **22**, **27**; Tudor Photography pp. **6**, **16**, **18**, **19**, **23**.

Cover photograph of children and height chart, reproduced with permission of Tudor Photography.

The publishers would like to thank Julie Johnson for her assistance in the preparation of this book.

Every effort has been made to contact copyright holders of any material reproduced in this book. Any omissions will be rectified in subsequent printings if notice is given to the publishers.

CONTENTS

Words appearing in the text in bold, **like this**, are explained in the Glossary.

WHY SHOULD I LOOK AFTER MYSELF?

From the moment you are born until you become an adult, your body is growing and developing. The human body grows following a set pattern – from baby, to child, to adolescent (teenage years) to adult. Everyone who reaches adulthood has gone through these stages.

You are what you are partly because of the way your body is designed to grow. However, you are an individual, and the way you look after yourself affects the way your body grows, too. Three of the most vital things that affect your growth are eating a healthy diet, sleeping well and taking regular exercise, but other things are also important.

What you do and the way you take care of yourself have a real effect on your body. Athletes may be born with a talent for their sport, but they have to do a lot of training to succeed.

How do people grow?

Every living thing is made up of many tiny living parts, called **cells**. These are so small that you can only see them through a microscope. Different types of cells carry out different jobs and form different parts of your body.

A baby is born after growing inside its mother for about nine months. Cells continue to divide for about eighteen years. Then you become an adult and stop growing.

A baby starts to grow when two very tiny cells – an **egg** from the mother and a **sperm** from the father – join to become a single cell. This new cell grows and divides into two. These two new cells, in turn, grow and divide into two more cells… and so on. This process is called cell division. At first, the new cells are all alike but, gradually, different kinds of cells form to become the different parts of the baby's body.

How does my body know how big to grow?

Hormones control many of the things that happen in your body. Growth hormones control the speed at which you grow and the way in which you grow. Hormones are like special messengers that travel around in the blood to the different parts of the body. When a growth hormone reaches a **cell**, it either enters it or sticks to its surface. The cell reacts to the growth hormone by starting to grow and divide.

The pituitary gland, which is located in your brain, is the **gland** that produces your growth hormones. It releases carefully measured doses of growth hormone into your bloodstream, so your body knows how big to grow.

Growth hormones tell your body how to grow. Most people increase in size by about 20 times between birth and adulthood!

If my parents are tall, will I be, too?

Most people end up somewhere between the height of their parents so, if your parents are tall, it is likely that you will be, too. The reason for this is that your body **inherits** its **genes** from your two parents. Genes are a special code contained in each body cell that instructs it how to grow. They are passed on when the **sperm** from your father joins with an **egg** inside your mother to form that first new cell that became you. As you grow, every new cell contains the same genes.

Genes also determine your eye, hair and skin colour – and even what kind of person you are. Some traits will come from your father, some from your mother and, in some aspects, you may resemble neither!

Scientists think that if you do not get enough sleep, you will not grow as tall as your genes intended you to.

WHY IS MY BODY CHANGING?

There are two times in your life when your body grows especially rapidly. The first time is in your first year of life – when you change from a baby into a child. The second is at **puberty** – when your body begins to change and develop to help you to become an adult instead of a child.

When does puberty happen?

No one can say exactly when your body will start to grow and change through puberty – there is no right time for puberty to begin. It usually starts earlier for girls than for boys. Girls may start puberty at any time between eight and fourteen years old, while boys may start puberty between ten and seventeen years old.

The stage in your life when you go through the process of puberty is also known as adolescence. Everyone goes through it – it is part of growing up.

What causes puberty?

Hormones cause the changes that happen during puberty. Your brain instructs your pituitary **gland** to send puberty hormones into your bloodstream. These puberty hormones travel to different parts of your body, so they begin to grow and change.

WHAT IS A GROWTH SPURT?

One of the first signs of puberty for boys and girls is a growth spurt – when your body grows fast. This growth spurt happens to bring you up to your adult height. During this time, you might grow up to 15 centimetres in one year! Your arms, legs, hands and feet may grow a bit faster than the rest of your body.

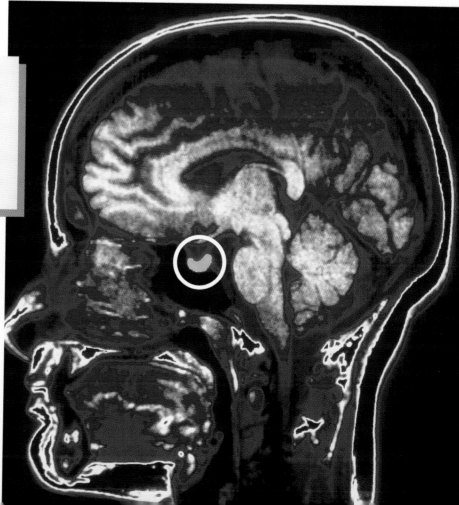

This is the pituitary gland – the pea-sized gland in your brain that controls your growth before and during puberty.

How do boys change?

If you are a boy, you will find that as you grow taller during **puberty**, your body changes in other ways, too. Your shoulders get broader, you may get heavier and your muscles get bigger. You will also notice your penis getting bigger and your testicles growing larger. These changes are all perfectly normal.

You will also find that hair starts to grow under your arms, on your legs and face, and around your penis. Some young men also grow chest hair. When you are older, you may decide to shave the hair on your face. Your skin starts to get oilier and you sweat more than you used to. This is because the sweat and oil glands in your skin are growing, too.

These choirboys are singing soprano – high notes. During puberty, boys' voices 'break' and become deeper. These boys will become tenors and basses – singing deeper notes.

How do girls change?

During puberty, a girl's body changes, too – you get a rounder tummy, hips and legs, and your breasts start to grow. You start to grow hair under your arms, in the pubic area (between your legs), and the hair on your legs may get thicker or darker. Like boys, your skin may get oilier and you will sweat more.

Some time during puberty, girls also start to menstruate (have a period). Each month, your body releases **egg cells** into your womb (the place where a baby can grow when you are an adult). To prepare for the egg, a lining of **tissue** and blood cells builds up in the womb. When these are not needed, they are released through your **vagina**. This is your period. It can last between two and seven days.

When you menstruate, you wear special pads to catch your period, so you can carry on life as normal.

WHY AM I SO HUNGRY?

As people grow, the amounts and kinds of food their body needs changes. In their first few months, babies only drink milk, but they have to feed every few hours. You have another growth spurt near **puberty**, and you get hungry at this age because you need extra food and a mixture of **nutrients** to fuel this growth.

How does food fuel growth?

Your body grows by making new **cells**. The **energy** to make new cells comes from your food. The best kinds of food for energy are **carbohydrates**. **Proteins** are the body-building food. When you eat protein-rich foods, your body breaks them down and uses the proteins to build body parts, such as muscles and skin.

These are some of the foods that are rich in protein. Dairy products, such as milk and cheese, are also important, because they contain calcium, which is vital for strong bones and teeth.

A balanced diet

Carbohydrates and proteins are not the only nutrients you need to be healthy. The plate below shows the different foods you need.

WHY EAT THREE MEALS A DAY?

People try to eat three meals a day because it is healthier to eat regularly. Make time to sit down and enjoy a healthy meal. For snacks, choose healthy, filling foods, such as fruit or bagels, rather than chocolate or crisps.

Include a carbohydrate in every meal, and eat at least five different fruit or vegetables a day. You only need to eat small amounts of protein-rich foods, two or three times a day. Fats, oils and sweets are useful foods, but only in very tiny amounts. One of the most important nutrients of all is water – try to drink six glasses a day.

The plate shows the proportions you need to eat of the different food groups.

13

WHY SHOULD I TAKE EXERCISE?

Doing some kind of physical activity (exercise) every day is an important part of helping your body to grow healthily. Exercise is especially important for young people, because it helps to strengthen bones and muscles as they grow.

How does exercise help?

Having strong muscles means that you can be active for longer. Strong muscles also protect you from injuries, because they give better support to your joints – the parts that link bones so you can bend and move. Bones are living, growing parts, with their own **blood vessels** and **nerves**, and they need exercise, too. Without regular movement, your bones can become brittle – that means they break more easily and cannot cope so well with everyday demands.

It is essential to build strong bones when you near **puberty**, because it is during this growth spurt that your bones grow strongest and thickest.

Other benefits

Doing regular exercise is also good for keeping your whole body fit and well. Activities that make you breathe harder, such as cycling or swimming, are called aerobic exercises. They give your heart and lungs a workout, and make these important body parts stronger and healthier. Doing sports is also a great way to make new friends or to meet up with old ones. It gives you a sense of achievement, not just when you win a match, but when you improve or play well.

It does not really matter what kind of exercise you do – just enjoy it and try to do some at least three or four times a week.

IDEAS FOR ACTIVITIES

Alone: skipping, dancing, cycling, walking, jogging, kite flying, cleaning the car, vacuuming.

Team sports: football, volleyball, basketball, baseball, netball – the list is endless.

Indoors: swimming, gymnastics, ice-skating, martial arts.

WHAT ARE GROWING PAINS?

Have you ever had pains in your legs, just when it is bedtime and you are trying to get to sleep? If you have, you were probably feeling 'growing pains'. This is not a kind of disease or a serious problem, but something lots of young people get at your age.

Why do I get growing pains?

Between the ages of eight and twelve years, you are growing fast, and your bones and muscles are changing as you get taller and stronger. Doctors believe that young people get growing pains when they have been busy running, climbing and jumping during the day, and that these growing muscles are simply tired out. Most people get growing pains around the muscles in their legs.

Growing pains often happen in the front of your thighs, in your calves (the backs of your legs below your knees) or behind your knees.

One way of dealing with growing pains is to do something else, such as read a book, to take your mind off them.

How can I soothe growing pains?

There are several ways to soothe growing pains. You can hold a heat pad or a hot water bottle against your leg. You can massage (rub) the leg, or gently stretch it. If it is really painful, you may need to ask an adult if you should have a mild painkiller – a medicine to ease the pain. Do not let growing pains put you off doing exercise – exercising regularly should reduce the risk of growing pains, because it makes your muscles stronger.

TAKE CARE

Most growing pains come at bedtime and have disappeared by the morning. If you have other kinds of pain, or pain that does not ease after a short time, you should always see a doctor to get it checked out.

WHY DO MY ARMPITS SMELL?

Some people choose to use underarm deodorants when they start to sweat more. Do not worry about this too much – having some body scents is perfectly normal.

Many young people notice that, as they get older, parts of their body, and especially their armpits, start to smell different. The smell is body odour (sometimes called BO for short), and it is perfectly natural.

What causes body odour?

As you near **puberty**, the hair that starts to grow under your armpits catches the increased amount of sweat that your body is making. The sweat gathers on the hair and becomes stale. **Bacteria** live on old sweat, and start to smell when they rot. This is what causes the smell. The only way to prevent body odour is to take a bath or shower every day, either before you go to bed or in the morning.

Why does my skin feel greasy?

Natural oils that collect on the skin and go stale can also cause body smells. As you reach puberty, **sebaceous glands** in the skin become more active. These are glands that make oil to help keep your skin and hair supple and waterproof. An increased amount of oil can cause spots and make your skin feel greasy. The answer is to take a bath or shower every day, and to wash with warm, soapy water and a clean sponge. Washing also gets rid of dirt on the skin, which may also smell if it is not washed off.

Another important part of looking after your body is cleaning your teeth. Brush them gently for two minutes twice a day. This is also a good time to start using dental floss to remove some of the bits of food that get trapped between your teeth. Cleaning your teeth regularly keeps your mouth smelling fresh.

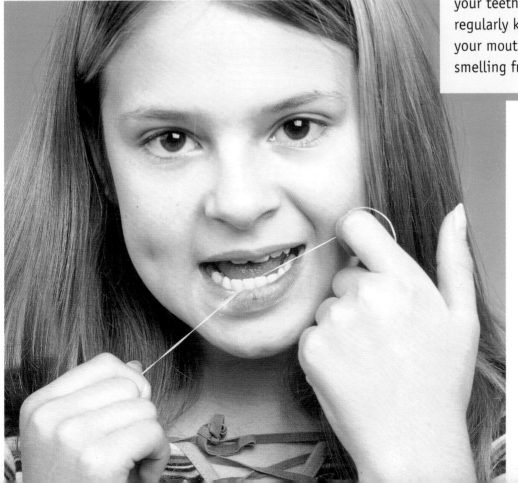

WHY SHOULD I WEAR A CYCLE HELMET?

Every year, thousands of cyclists suffer head injuries that could have been prevented by wearing helmets.

Cyclists of all ages should wear a helmet but, when you were little, your parents put it on – now it is up to you. As you grow up, you begin to do things and to go places on your own, so you have to take responsibility for looking after your body.

Staying safe

Many children are injured every year because of bad choices. Some are injured when they dive into shallow water. Some get hurt when they fool about with gardening or DIY tools. Of course, as you learn new skills, there may be some risks. As you learn to cook, you may burn yourself or, as you learn a new sport, you may hurt your leg. The important thing is to act sensibly and to avoid unnecessary risks.

How can I make healthy choices?

To be safe, think about what risks are involved with an activity. When you learn a new sport, find out what safety gear you need – and wear it. Learn the rules of the road so you can be safe when you go out and about. Make sure an adult is with you if you use tools or other equipment that may be dangerous.

Looking after yourself means making choices that keep you safe and healthy – such as always crossing the road safely.

RULES OF THE ROAD

Many young people are killed on roads every year when they start to travel to and from school alone. Wear bright clothes or reflective strips when it is dark. Use pedestrian crossings to cross the road when you can, and always pause to check if a car is coming before you cross.

WHAT IS WRONG WITH SMOKING?

When people smoke, it damages **cells** in their lungs. This can cause cancer. The red area in this picture is lung cancer. At least one in every two people who smoke will die early because of the cigarettes.

To grow up healthy, you need to avoid picking up bad habits – and smoking is one of them. Smoking can cause serious and life-threatening health problems later in life, such as bronchitis, heart disease and cancer. Before that, cigarettes will stain your teeth, make your breath, hair and clothes smell, cost you a lot of money, make your skin dry and cause lung problems that affect your breathing.

What is an addiction?

If you start smoking, it can become very addictive, which means that it is hard to stop doing it. Cigarettes are so damaging to health that cigarette and tobacco packets and publicity have to carry health warnings.

What are drugs?

Drugs are substances that affect your mind or body. Some drugs are useful, such as the medicines a doctor gives to people to make them well – as long as they take the correct amount. Other drugs, such as alcohol, cigarettes, illegal drugs and inhalants (aerosols and glue), can be very bad for your health and very addictive.

Some people think that smoking makes them look cool and grown-up. In fact, it is far more mature to say no when you are offered a cigarette!

What if it is hard to say no?

Peer pressure is when you do something because your friends tell you to or expect you to. As you grow up, you have to make your own decisions about caring for your body. Make it easier by avoiding situations where drugs, such as alcohol or cigarettes, are present. Choose friends who also do  not use these substances. Be confident that you know what is best for the health of your growing body.

WHY DO I FEEL ANGRY SOMETIMES?

As you get older and grow up, **hormones** are not only busy changing the way your body looks on the outside, but they also create changes on the inside, too. These changes affect the way you feel about yourself and other people, so that you may find that you feel confused, easily upset or angrier more often than you used to.

Many young people get upset because they feel anxious about their changing bodies.

Part of growing up is starting to separate more from your parents. This makes some people feel angry and rebellious – they argue with parents or carers, or go against adult advice. Feeling rebellious is a natural part of growing up, but do not let these feelings tempt you to do things that are really bad for you, such as smoking, taking drugs or drinking alcohol.

How should I deal with these feelings?

Sometimes it is hard to deal with these emotions. When you have a bad day, try to remember that you have these feelings because you are adjusting to all the changes taking place in your growing body. It is perfectly normal to feel this way – and it is not your 'fault'.

One of the most important things to do is talk about what you are feeling. Do not bottle up your emotions. That will only make you feel worse.

It also helps to take care of your body at this time. Make sure that you get a good night's sleep, because lack of sleep can make you feel worse. Exercise is good, too. As well as making you feel good, exercise helps you to relax. You may feel fired up straight afterwards, but exercise helps you to relax and sleep better later.

WHY DO I NEED CHECK-UPS?

WHAT ARE MEDICINES?

Medicines are chemicals. Some come from plants or animals, and others are made artificially in laboratories. Antibiotics are medicines that fight the **germs** that cause illness. Antibiotics only fight illnesses caused by **bacteria**. They do not cure illnesses caused by **viruses**, such as the common cold.

You need to take care of your growing body. If you get ill, or have a headache, rash or pain that does not go away quickly, you should see your doctor. If the doctor prescribes a medicine to make you better, only take the amount they tell you to. Never share medicines or take drugs that a doctor has not prescribed, apart from mild painkillers an adult might give you.

When you get sick, it is probably because germs have got into your body. Antibiotics can kill the germs so you can get better.

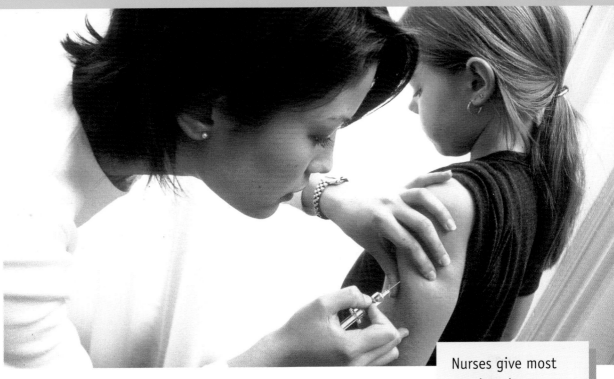

What are vaccines?

Vaccines are medicines that help you to grow up healthy by preventing you from catching some serious diseases. A vaccine contains a small amount of dead or harmless versions of a particular disease. These cannot make you ill, but they can help your body to make antibodies, which defend your body against the disease. These antibodies stay in your blood for a long time, ready to defend your body if you catch the real disease.

Nurses give most vaccines by injection. They insert a fine needle under the skin and inject the vaccine into your bloodstream. It is then carried all around your body. Lots of people feel nervous about injections, but they do not hurt too much.

Although vaccines cannot give you the disease they are meant to prevent, you may feel a bit grotty for a day or so after you have them. This is normal, and is nothing to worry about.

27

Think of your body as a machine, such as a bicycle. Its different parts need regular checking to keep them in good condition.

What other check-ups do I need?

As well as visiting the doctor when you are ill or a nurse when you need a vaccine, you should also have check-ups for your teeth, eyes and ears. Dentists recommend that you have a check-up every six months. This means that tooth decay and gum disease can be spotted early, and treated before too much damage is done.

You should have your eyes checked by an optician once a year. As well as checking your eyesight, opticians can provide you with glasses or contact lenses to correct poor vision.

Although most people do not have regular hearing check-ups, you should always have your hearing checked if you think that your hearing does not work as well as it used to.

GROWTH AND DEVELOPMENT

Everybody grows to a set pattern. First, you are a
baby, then you become a toddler, then a child,
then an adolescent, then an adult and,
finally, you reach old age.

GLOSSARY

bacteria tiny living things that can cause disease

blood vessels tubes carrying blood around your body

carbohydrates kind of food that gives you energy

cells tiny building blocks of all living things

egg cell produced by a female which, when joined with a sperm cell from a male, can grow into a baby

energy energy allows living things to do everything they need to live and grow

genes information in all living things that determines the way they are

germs tiny living things that can cause disease

glands parts of the body that produce hormones or other chemicals

hormone chemical that controls body processes

inherit pass on something from parent to child

nerves nerves carry messages to and from the brain

nutrients kinds of chemicals found in food that we need to be healthy

proteins foods that our bodies use to build body parts

puberty stage in life when your body rapidly develops to become an adult instead of a child

sebaceous glands skin glands that make oil

sperm cell produced by a male which, when joined with an egg cell, can grow into a baby

tissues groups of cells that do the same job

vagina passage between the uterus (womb), where a baby can grow, and the outside of a female body

viruses tiny living things that cause diseases

FURTHER READING

Growing Up, Kate Brookes (Hodder Children's Books, 2000)

Growing Up, Sally Hewitt (Franklin Watts, 2001)

What Do You Know About Puberty and Growing Up, Pete Sanders and S. Myers (Franklin Watts, 2000)

INDEX